HOW TO BUILD A
ROCK
SOLID
MARRIAGE

Choices That Will Give You
The Marriage Of Your
Dreams

TONY PETERS

Published by

T.P.PUBLICATIONS

4 Pegamoid Road. Edmonton.
London. N18 2NG.

www.rocksolidmarriages.com

HOW TO BUILD A
ROCK SOLID MARRIAGE

CONTENT

DEDICATION

I
Dedicate this
Book To All Who Read it
And To My Wife & Best Friend,
Shola Peters

INTRODUCTION

For the LORD God is a sun and shield; the LORD will give grace and glory; no good thing will He withhold from those who walk uprightly.   (Psalms 84:11.)

No one getting married ever plans to have a bad marriage. However, if you don't intentionally put some effort into nurturing a rock solid marriage, you are planning to fail by default. That's why the journey you are about to embark upon in this book is so crucial.

You see, good marriages don't just happen. In every marriage, there are mindsets that need to be corrected, choices that need to be made, commitments that need to be embraced, and actions that need to be modified.

Every happily married couple had to embrace change at some point in their relationship for them to stay happily married. They had to take proactive steps towards keeping their marriage strong and on course.

Whenever you see a marriage relationship fail, it's almost always because these indispensable undertakings were either not made at all, or if they were made, the couple failed to follow through on them.

So regardless of what life throws at you or your marriage, I want you to know that your marriage can eventually develop staying power. You can have the marriage of your dreams and more.

The first step towards building a rock solid marriage is to really want one to start with. Many couples start out just hoping that things will be okay; all things being equal. Well, all things are not equal - so things start to fall apart for them.

Successful couples, however, know that things don't always happen the way they want them to happen. They understand that things tend to decay if left uncared for and unkempt. So they plan ahead of time to nurture their marriage so that it doesn't decay too.

I trust that you are reading this book because you know that you'll need to play a crucial part in nurturing the kind of marriage you want.

The second step towards building a rock solid marriage is to discover the choices and commitments you need to make to give your marriage the chance it needs to succeed. You are already taking this step by taking time to read this book.

Finally, you would need to develop the tenacity, fortitude and maturity to follow through on your commitments. Your chances of succeeding will even quadruple, if both you and your spouse can make and take these three steps together.

Each chapter will cover a different set of commitments. As you read through each concept, don't just browse through; make sure you take time to reflect on how you would go about making and keeping that commitment in your relationship.

If you've already made the commitment, take time to reflect on how you can strengthen it by consistently executing it, irrespective of the challenges you may be facing in other aspects of your relationship.

In other words, you are not going to get the results you want because you **know** what's right, but because you **do** the right things that you know.

A word of caution here: Don't make the mistake of thinking that you can keep your commitments to your spouse or to your marriage with your will power or self-reliance. No, you need God's help and a lot of prayers. That way, you'll be able to stay on course.

You will also find inner strength to control your ego and pride if you draw more on God's unlimited help.

Marriage is God's idea. God intended for us to do everything we can to make our marriages work. You need to believe – with every fibre of your being – that when God said He hates divorce[1], He really meant it. You have to believe that He wants you to hate it too.

As you tuck into the first chapter of this book, all that remains is for me to assure you that God is eager to help you succeed in your marriage. I say this because when you do succeed, God will get the glory; other couples around you will be encouraged; and you would enjoy life as God intended.

So, let the journey begin!

[1] Malachi 2:16.

1

FIVE PRECEPTS THAT GIVE YOU PERSPECTIVE IN MARRIAGE

"And you shall know the truth, and the truth shall make you free." (John 8:32.)

Although I may not know you personally, I know that most people who get married need to make some mindset adjustments because of the lies and myths we've all believed and embraced over the years. Even those of us who've been married for years still often need to make these paradigm shifts to improve on the quality of our marriages.

Here are five truths I teach people to help them see some aspects of their married life in perspective. If you embrace them and let them form the grid through which you evaluate the ups and downs of your marriage, you will not go wrong.

1. You live in a broken world and people are not perfect

Understand that things are never going to be perfect while you are functioning in this side of heaven. Your spouse – no matter how much he or she tries – is going to make mistakes. You too are going to get things wrong from time to time, whether you like it or not.

Even when both of you are sure that you are right about something, don't be surprised to discover that one or both of you might be wrong. Why? Because you are both flawed people living in an imperfect world. You are mortal beings and you are both still 'work in progress'.

For instance, there was a time in history when everybody thought the earth was flat; and they would have put you in jail for postulating anything different. But alas! They were all wrong.

I like a particular definition of marriage because it highlights this point very well. It says: **Marriage is an unconditional commitment to spend the rest of your life with an imperfect person.** How insightful! If people only knew this, and took its implication to heart, they would be less critical and more forgiving.

The good news, however, is that imperfect people can be loving and caring. Flawed mortals can grow to be merciful. Both you and your spouse can learn to forgive. And, you don't need to be perfect to be kind either.

If you would only make this slight adjustment to your thinking, a lot of unnecessary pain, conflict and disappointment will be avoided. You will stop expecting perfection and start expressing more empathy and understanding.

So never forget that you live in a broken world and that your spouse is not perfect. There again, neither are you!

2. The challenges you face in your relationship are there to make you and your marriage stronger

You've got to believe that trials and conflicts are the 'emotional dumbbells' God uses to build your spiritual and relational muscles. No marriage can get stronger and indestructible without its fair share of them. Just like your physical muscles need pressure and exercise to grow stronger, your marital 'biceps' need a healthy dose of conflicts to peak.

The Bible expresses this truth in these words:

> **Dear brothers and sisters, whenever trouble comes your way, let it be an opportunity for joy. For when your faith is tested, your endurance has a chance to grow. So let it grow, for when your endurance is fully developed, you will be strong in character and ready for anything.**
>
> (James 1:2-4.) NLT

Notice, what this passage is saying. It is saying that trials are good for you, if you learn endurance through them and allow them to build your character. In short, challenges are opportunities for joy and growth.

The challenges you experience in your relationship will only serve to make you a better, wiser and more stable person once you understand that this was the reason for the challenge in the first place.

I don't know any strong marriage that did not go through its fair share of challenges. But I also don't know any weak or failed marriage that believed in and embraced this concept wholeheartedly.

So, start to believe from today that the challenges you face in your relationship are serving a good purpose and will in-time make you and your marriage much stronger.

Remember also that, **God causes everything to work together for the good of those who love Him and who are called according to his purposes for them.**[1] 'Everything' here includes the challenges and setbacks you face in your marriage.

3. No effort you put into preparing yourself for the marriage you want is wasted

Another shift you have to make in your thinking and in your behaviour is to do with the deception that your marriage development is the responsibility of someone else. It's yours; and the sooner you accept it, the quicker you can start to invest in the future you were created to enjoy.

The law of 'cause and effect' works well here. This law says that you can never really get something for nothing. That's especially true when it comes to relationships. Experience proves that those who put in the effort, the time and the sacrifice are best placed to reap the results they passionately desire. The Bible illustrates this truth succinctly like so:

> **"Do not be deceived; God is not mocked, for whatever a man sows, that he will also reap."**
> (Galatians 6:7.)

It's a divine law that can't be broken. Therefore, never get weary of learning how relationships work. Never stop reading good books. Never stop attending good relational seminars or workshops. Never stop growing. Never stop improving your attitude or behaviour, because a great marriage is always worth any effort you put into it.

Since 'reaping what you sow' is an unbreakable law of life, the time, effort and determination you invest in your marriage would eventually pay off. When it does, you'll be glad you didn't leave it to chance.

So work on your marriage like it's all you've got. If you would invest yourself in it and devote yourself to its success, you cannot fail to enjoy the rewards of your labour. You cannot fail to build yourself a rock solid marriage.

4. Great marriages are made on earth, not in heaven

Rock solid marriages that give us a foretaste of heaven on earth are forged in the furnace of unconditional love, forgiveness, understanding, commitment and sacrifice. There is no simpler way!

If you want a fulfilling marriage, you must be committed to the hard work of getting to know and love your spouse. You must be willing to embrace an attitude of humility and selflessness. You must learn to forgive 'seventy times seven times' a day. And, you must develop the determination not to give up when the going is tough.

You see, you'd be tempted to look over the fence of your life and conclude that 'the grass is greener on the other side'. But the people on the other side don't think their grass is green at all. They are more likely to wonder why their grass is brown in the middle of spring. So what you are seeing is really an illusion.

You must also drop all those fairytale ideas that great marriages are made in heaven. They are not. Heaven may sanction your marriage, but you and your partner are going to have to build it on earth with your sweat and blood.

You have to want a great marriage. You have to design it; you have to construct it with the raw materials you've been given; and you have to fight 'tooth and nail' to keep your marriage away from the enemy's evil claws.

Of course, God promises to help you along the way, but you have to ask for it sincerely and tenaciously. Then, you would have to cooperate with the help you get from above, when it's given.

> **"Keep on asking, and you will receive what you ask for. Keep on seeking, and you will find. Keep on knocking, and the door will be opened to you. For everyone who asks, receives. Everyone who seeks, finds. And to everyone who knocks, the door will be opened."**
>
> (Matthew 7:7-8.) Amplified

A great marriage is the result of a great vision, a great desire and a great character. If you have all three, nothing can stop you from landing a rock solid marriage sooner or later.

5. You are equipped to succeed in any Godly endeavour you embark upon

Yes you are! You need to carry this conviction everywhere you go. If you are connected to God (through His Only

Begotten Son, Jesus Christ) and if you are committed to following His instructions, you have a blood-bought right to succeed in your marriage. God says it this way:

"Study this Book of Instruction continually. Meditate on it day and night so you will be sure to obey everything written in it. Only then will you prosper and succeed in all you do."

(Joshua 1:8.) NLT

Notice, God says it's possible to prosper and succeed in *all* you do. Not in a few easy things you do, but in *all* you do. And that includes your marriage.

Knowing that you are equipped to win in life is so crucial when it comes to marriage, because many of the obstacles you experience will try to tell you otherwise.

That's why the Apostle Paul was bold enough to declare, **"I can do all things through Christ who strengthens me."** [2]

You must know deep within your heart that you <u>can</u> do all things through Christ who strengthens you; that you <u>can</u> have a rock solid marriage; that you <u>can</u> be the ideal spouse; that you <u>can</u> satisfy and fulfil your partner; and that you <u>can</u> handle everything life throws at you with dignity and confidence.

God literally resides in your heart. So you shouldn't fail to achieve what you desire in your marriage, because the God who resides in you is not a failure.

In short, you must know, *that you know,* that you are destined to win in your marriage. This is the kind of mindset that opens a bright future before you and that dramatically increases your chances of building a rock solid marriage.

Never forget that God's Word is what equips you to succeed in every area of your life. Therefore, cherish it, read it, study it, meditate on it and obey it. You cannot do these things and still fail to construct the marriage of your dreams. I know that because your marriage would be built on the eternal foundation of God's word – which is an immovable anchor in the midst of the storms of life.

Don't leave Christ out of the Equation

As you prepare your heart to go the distance in your marriage, I am convinced that you and your spouse can learn to thrive and win the battles and the challenges ahead of you. If that were not so, Jesus' death and resurrection would be in vain.
Fortunately, Christ came to offer you a life filled with victories and triumphs. And He succeeded in His mission.

That's why I make bold to say that you are going to make it. Oh, I am not suggesting that you wouldn't face some real challenges – because you will. The broken world we live in guarantees that you will experience some tough times. What I am saying, though, is that a tight relationship with Christ will equip you to handle and overcome them.

You see, I've prayed for you and asked God to get a copy of this book into the hands of special people who would benefit maximally from it. I've also asked God to impart the grace that has been upon my life and marriage (for the last 25 years) upon yours too.

So, again, I make bold to say that you are going to succeed in your marriage. You will get out of it more than you imagined possible. And, your marriage is going to be as blissful and as beautiful as you sincerely desire it to be.

Declare the following statements out loud to yourself;

- **The challenges I face are there to make me and my relationship stronger**

- **No time or effort I put into improving my marriage or relationship is wasted**

- **I am equipped by God to succeed in any Godly endeavour I embark upon** (And my marriage is a Godly endeavour)

Before you read the next few pages of this book, I want you to get these truths into your head and heart. Personalise and repeat them to yourself until you can say a firm 'Yes!' to every one of them, and until you feel yourself developing faith for what you will be reading in the rest of this book.

[1] Romans 8:28.
[2] Philippians 4:13.

2

SEVEN RELATIONSHIP
KILLERS TO AVOID

"Do your part to live in peace with everyone, as much as possible." (Romans 12:18.) NLT.

As you embark on this journey to build a rock solid marriage, you must be careful not to tear down (with your own hands, so to speak) what you are trying to build. It is one thing to protect your marriage from outside forces, over which you have little control; but it is quite another thing to protect your marriage from 'inward' mindsets, attitudes and behaviour, over which you do have substantial control.

So, I want to highlight seven **'inward' enemies** of a rock solid marriage. I call them 'inward' enemies because they come from deep within us, and they are products of our thought patterns, our values, our fears, our insecurities, and even our upbringing.

1. The Urge To Control Or Change Your Spouse

Human beings were never created to be controlled. That's why two-year-old kids start to rebel against all forms of control, as soon as they can think for themselves. As we grow older, we get even more spiteful and aggressive towards any hints of domination. Again, that's why controlling relationships are never healthy.

God intentionally created us to be different and to prefer different things, so that when we come together in marriage, there would be variety. Yes, God designed us to function like the ivory and ebony keys of a grand piano. The keys are very different in colour and tune, but together they produce angelic music at the hands of the Master Player.

Therefore, one way to develop a great relationship with someone very different from you is to get excited about their uniqueness (who they are and what they like) and decide to be happy for them and for the variety they bring to the table.

"Let nothing be done through strife or vainglory, but in lowliness of mind let each esteem others better than themselves." (Philippians 2:3.)

For instance, my wife loves romantic and tender family friendly films. I like action-packed, car-chasing, building-exploding, machine-gun blasting block-busters. Happily, I learnt early in my marriage that I was not going to change my wife's film preference and she was not going to change mine.

So, instead of trying to change each other or allowing our difference to separate us, we learnt to be selfless. I learnt to enjoy (what I called) 'girly' films with my wife – so that we could be together; and she learnt to share in my adrenalin producing movies.

Controlling your spouse or trying to force him/her to do what you want is demeaning and humiliating. Your spouse may put up with it for a while to keep the peace, but lasting joy and satisfaction will evaporate under the scotching heat of 'control'.

Kill the urge to change or control your spouse before it kills your marriage. Your relationship will blossom when your goal is to please and pleasure your partner. But to do that you must understand that being controlling is always counter-productive and selfless-ness is always better.

2. The Need To Always Be Right, At Any Cost

The need to be 'right' at any cost is the Achilles heel of opinionated people. Your marriage will be toxic if you are always out to win the argument or be 'right'. Why? Because you are bruising your partner's ego by insinuating that he/she is always wrong. After all, if you are always 'right', your spouse, of necessity, must always be wrong.

If you keep doing this, what your spouse is constantly hearing is, "You are dumb", "You are unintelligent", "You are thick", and "We are not in the same league". Even if you are actually wiser or more intelligent, you must go out of your way to help your spouse see that he/she is not totally clueless or without a brain. Anything less is pride!

> **"Pride leads to destruction; humility leads to honour."** (Proverbs 18:12.) CEV.

In fact, if you really love your spouse, you would be looking for ways to elevate him/her, because your spouse, in the final analysis, is a reflection on you. Yes, your spouse is a reflection on you. After all, you chose, courted, and married this person.

If you keep projecting stupidity onto your spouse, you must be 'stupid' too for marrying him/her. Were you blind? Were you gagged? Did someone hold a gun to your head? I don't think so. My point is that your spouse is not what you are making him/her out to be.

Give your spouse's ideas a chance to succeed. Give him/her credit for some of the things they bring to the table. Don't sabotage good ideas to score points. Don't shut your spouse down because you are not in agreement with their ideas or because you feel yours are better. Also, don't shoot them down because you want to be 'right'.

Learn to be charitable enough to boost your spouse's confidence; by adopting his/her ideas and making them work. You can't do this if you are always right, or if you take all the decisions, or if you always insist on doing things your way.

Which is better: To be 'right' and miserable or to share in decision-making and be united? An unhappy marriage and an insecure spouse is too great a price to pay for being 'right'. If being 'right' is really right, it should lead to good things. If it's not, it's not really right.

So, kill the need to be right at any cost and you'd be surprised at how right your spouse can be if you put the effort you put into being 'right' into making sure that your spouse is secure and right too. If you understand the marriage vows you took, you will understand that it is your duty to build your spouse up, not to tear him/her down.

3. The Temptation To Retaliate And Not Forgive

Retaliation is a very human trait. When we've been offended, we feel bad and tell ourselves that we would feel better when our offender has been made to feel the pain we felt.

The truth, though, is that we often feel worst for retaliating, because it seldom takes away our pain. And, especially in marriage, it never really mends or heals anything. What heals is forgiveness. What heals our pain is love and kindness. What heals is learning to transform our negative energy into a positive one.

Fortunately, those of us who love God understand that He promises to level the score if we leave every offence committed against us in His capable hands.

Dear friends, never avenge yourselves. Leave that to God. For it is written, "I will take vengeance; I will repay those who deserve it," says the Lord. (Romans 12:19.) NLT.

When your spouse offends you remember that you have offended God a thousand times more, but He forgave you. So, learn to forgive and release your spouse into the hands of God. Never allow your actions to be controlled by your emotions.

Retaliation never accomplishes anything good anyway – only forgiveness does.

"If your brother sins against you, rebuke him; and if he repents, forgive him. And if he sins against you seven times in a day, and seven times in a day returns to you, saying, 'I repent,' you

shall forgive him." (Luke 17:3-4.)

One last word here: If your spouse's offences are intentional and continuous, go and get advice from a marriage counsellor or a respected minister. I don't think God wants you to suffer in silence; and I don't think forgiveness should prevent you from seeking help if things are getting out of hand. The crucial thing is that you are not looking to retaliate, because retaliation hurts you as well. And sometimes, it even hurts you the most.

4. The Urge To Criticise Far More Than You Encourage

Nobody wants to be criticised and belittled all the time. Yet we thoughtlessly do it to the people who are supposed to be the closest to us. It is wise to remember that everyone has something going on in their life for which they can be praised or encouraged.

In fact, encouragement is what helps us grow and improve. Constant criticism only makes us want to give up, as we feel there is nothing we can do to appease our critic. I'm sure you know the feeling. You do your best, but your best is not good enough for Mr. Never Satisfied.

My point is that your spouse needs to hear your encouraging words more than your critical ones. Resist the temptation to always evaluate your spouse. Resist the urge to dish out negative and critical comments every time you are not happy with something; because the spirit behind this attitude is often worst than the thing that is being criticised.
Even when your spouse is doing something you don't like, you don't have to verbalise it in a critical way again and

again. If you've said it a couple of time before, your spouse already knows how you feel about the issue.

If, on the other hand, you would spend your energy in praising and encouraging your spouse for the things he/she gets right, <u>two</u> things will happen in your marriage before long:

i.) **You'd start to see less of the things that used to bug you so much about your spouse** – because your attention and energy are now positively focused.

ii.) **Your spouse would start to put more effort into doing the things that attract your approval** – because your spouse (like the rest of us) values the praise and encouragement he/she gets from loved ones.

Do you find yourself constantly criticising and disapproving of your spouse's behaviour or choices? If you do, you must take steps to stop it, because it is a marriage killer. Criticising your spouse will stifle communication; it will smother openness; and it will breed destructive conflict.

In the end, a rock solid marriage can only be built on a rock solid foundation of acceptance, encouragement and positive affirmations.

> **"Let each of you look out not only for his own interests, but also for the interests of others."**
> (Philippians 2:4.)

5. **The Refusal To Communicate How You Are Feeling**

Too many married people feel that the best way to deal with a challenge in their relationship is to shut their spouse out for a season and respond with the dreaded 'silent treatment'. That's when one or both parties refuse to speak to each other for as long as possible. They generally avoid each other and try to keep the sum total of their discussion to the 'read-my-mind' level.

But the refusal to communicate in marriage is a really dangerous strategy because, while it is often deployed to reduce the conflict at hand, it actually allows the conflict to grow into a monster.

The longer the silent treatment lasts, the more difficult it gets for the couple to talk about their pain and reconcile. As a result, lots of hurts get swept under the proverbial 'rug' and the hurts continue to fester in the dark recesses of their heart.

This destructive behaviour allows the couple to exaggerate the conflict, embellish the hurts, overstate the damage done, and make permanent decisions over temporary challenges. The enemy of your marriage just loves it when you don't communicate because it's a lose-lose game for you and a win-win game for him.

When you don't speak to your spouse after a relational setback, two things happen: **Firstly,** you internalise and incubate toxic feelings that can eventually affect your health adversely. **Secondly,** you deprive your spouse of an opportunity to apologise, explain, or understand how you are feeling.

If you have to retreat after a conflict to evaluate what happened so that your response can be measured and appropriate, that is good. But endeavour to keep the communication lines open as soon as humanly possible.

My wife and I decided earlier on in our marriage to sort out our arguments and quarrels before we went to bed. That means that we rarely went more than twenty-four hour before we sat down to talk. Well, that's precisely what God's Word instructs couples to do.

"And don't sin by letting anger gain control over you. Don't let the sun go down while you are still angry, for anger gives a mighty foothold to the Devil." (Ephesians 4:26-27.) NLT.

Sadly, too many couples give Satan an avoidable foothold into their lives because they wouldn't follow this divine injunction. And, the results are devastating. I know, because I had an aunt who had a massive stroke because she allegedly kept too many painful experiences bottled up.

Irrespective of the type of temperament you have, you must learn to share what you are feeling with your spouse in a mature and positive way. If you don't, you risk hurting yourself by keeping alive the very thing that's hurting you. So keep your lines of communication open, when you are tempted to shut them down.

Finally, if talking to your spouse about your concerns is proving unproductive, find a helpful minister or marriage counsellor to talk to. Never keep the hurts and disappointments of your relationship hidden, because they are poisonous and toxic to your health and wellbeing.

When matters of the heart are brought out into the light, they lose their sting, their poison, and their power. When they are kept in the dark, they grow into unpredictable monsters that attempt to consume you.

6. The Temptation To Respond To Issues In An Unbridled Manner

When you are upset with your spouse, you'd be tempted to give him/her a piece of your mind – usually the offensive piece. But I want to advice you not to act or speak so quickly because words spoken in anger and actions taken in haste cannot be taken back easily.

Always ask yourself whether the things you want to say will make things better or worst. Will they harm or heal? Will they pacify or will they enrage your spouse? Ask yourself whether you'd regret saying it or whether you'd be pleased that you said it, when things get better between you.

In a troubled marriage, words are often more lethal than physical abuse because they go deeper. They hack at the soul; they the lacerate the ego; and they damage human dignity and self-esteem.

That's why the Word of God instructs us to watch what we say.

> **"When you talk, do not say harmful things, but say what people need—words that will help them become stronger. Then what you say will do good to those who listen to you."**
>
> (Ephesians 4:29.) NCV.

As a Christian, it is your duty to exercise self-control. You are not an instinctive animal designed to respond to every challenge intuitively. You have the power of choice. You can choose how you respond to each challenge and conflict that confronts you. So, choose to respond to your spouse in love.

"... Above all things have fervent love for one another, for love will cover a multitude of sins."
(1 Peter 4:8.)

In times of conflict and disagreement, choose to speak and act like a person who knows that you have God living on the inside of you. That's your prerogative! That's what it means to be a follower of Christ.

The temptation to act in an unbridled and uncontrolled manner is a double-edged sword. It will hurt you as much, if not more, than it hurts your spouse. If you find yourself getting so upset or angry that you blow your top, know that you are sinning against God and against your spouse. Repent and make amends; and watch God transform your marriage because of your commitment to do the right thing.

7. The Habit Of Digging Up Past Hurts And Wounds

Another very common relationship killer is the addictive habit of digging up past hurts and issues that should have been forgiven and 'forgotten'. As Christians, God expects us to really forgive people who hurt us – especially when they've asked to be forgiven.

"For if ye forgive men their trespasses, your heavenly Father will also forgive you. But if ye

forgive not men their trespasses, neither will your Father forgive your trespasses."

(Matthew 6:14-15.)

Bringing up past hurts again and again is like peeling the scab off an old wound that's trying to heal. Instead of healing, the wound bleeds afresh and the healing process has to start from scratch again.

Digging up past offences only proves to your spouse that you are still holding on to these hurts. It also complicates the business of reconciliation and will tend to make your spouse defensive and less apologetic. This is because your partner is likely to feel that you are being unfair and vindictive.

When people dig up past hurts, it is usually to justify their anger or bad behaviour; or to shame their spouse into admitting failure. Either way, it is harmful and unfair to your spouse.

If you must 'fight' with your partner, at least learn to 'fight' fair. Learn to deal with the issue at hand alone. Learn to keep the discussion simple, current and to the point.

"So then, let us aim for *peace and* harmony... and try to build each other up." (Romans 14:19.)

If you've developed the habit of resurrecting past hurts and failures whenever you have a quarrel with you partner, stop it!

Now, I know that it is not the easiest thing to do, especially when your spouse keeps doing the same things that caused conflict in the past. Nevertheless, if your partner has asked

30

for your forgiveness, you must decide to draw a line under the issue, bite your lips and never bring them up again.

Finally, if you'd take the care to avoid these seven 'relationship killers' in your marriage, you would be well on your way to building a rock solid marriage that would inspire and encourage generations to come.

If you are a child of God, it is your right to have a great marriage because your Daddy instituted it. So draw on God's grace today and go for gold! You've got what it takes!!

3

MASTERING THE ART
OF GOOD COMMUNICATION

"A good person produces good words from a good heart, and an evil person produces evil words from an evil heart. And I tell you this, that you must give an account on judgment day of every idle word you speak. The words you say now reflect your fate then; either you will be justified by them or you will be condemned by them." (Matthew 12:35-37.) NLT

Communication is the tool God gives us to share our thoughts, concerns and dreams in an unselfish manner with our partners. It is the lifeline of your marriage. It is the bridge that connects your heart to the heart of your spouse. Communication will make you vulnerable with your partner, but it cannot be avoided if you want to stay married.

When communication in the marriage is healthy, the marriage is healthy. So, if you want to build a rock solid marriage, you must endeavour to grow in your ability to communicate well with your spouse.

Men and women communicate differently because we are wired differently. It is not wise for women to expect their husbands to communicate with them the way other women do – because men are not generally wired that way. Similarly, men should not expect their wives to be satisfied with the surface quality of communication that they have with other men – because women generally need more.

One of the sure signs that a marriage is heading for trouble is when it starts to lack positive, encouraging and affirming communication. The couple either stop speaking to each other altogether; or they speak harshly, disrespectfully or condescendingly to each other at the slightest opportunity. Typically, one harsh comment by either spouse is followed by a more demeaning comment by the other. And this can go on until the atmosphere between them is thick with hatred and revulsion.

But this does not have to be the case with you and your partner. You can both learn better and more positive ways to express yourselves. You can also learn how to make allowances for those differences between you and your spouse; and deflect away unhealthy communication 'bugs'.

Let's examine some precepts that should help increase your ability to communicate better with your spouse.

1.) **Communication does not end with Speaking.**

The circle of good communication covers talking, listening, understanding and acting on what was communicated. Just because you've said something doesn't mean that you effectively communicated with the intended recipient.

A year ago, while I was doing some shopping in Italy, a seller was passionately trying to tell or sell me something, but I didn't understand a word of what he was saying. He was speaking a language I didn't understand. He was talking; he was passionate; but he was not communicating.

The same is true in marriage. Your spouse may hear what you said, but not interpret it the way you meant it. That's why it is important to check that your spouse is on the same page with you during a serious discussion.

One way to do this is to respectfully ask your spouse to repeat to you – in his/her own words – what they believe you've been saying. That way, you will be able to correct any misunderstanding and affirm that your communication was successful. If you do this, you would avoid tons of conflict.

2.) Communication is not a Science, it's an Art.

The way a person communicates is a composite of upbringing, training, conditioning, personality, circumstance and language comprehension. And, none of these parts are the same for any two people. That's perhaps the reason why so many of us struggle with understanding others.

Therefore, it's important to realise that good communication with your spouse will not happen overnight. Even after 25 years of marriage, my wife and I continually work on the way we communicate. The truth is that I am changing all the time and so is my wife. So we keep learning and adapting and forgiving each other because we are committed to communicating in a healthy way.

"For we all make many mistakes, and if any one

makes no mistakes in what he says he is a perfect man, able to bridle the whole body also." (James 3:2.)

The point being, that communication is complex and the results can be very unpredictable. Nevertheless, you can get better at communicating with time, even if you never quite hit perfection. I trust that the principles in the rest of this chapter will help.

3.) Constant Miscommunication often leads to Severe Consequences

I cannot count how many times my wife and I have said things to each other only to find out later that a miscommunication had occurred. Usually, these lead to hurtful and painful consequences. Sometimes they lead to tears or frustration or even anger.

The reason for this is simple. Words are powerful. They can build and they can destroy. They can encourage and they can discourage. They can motivate and they can cripple. They have the power to heal or to wound. That's why you cannot afford to be careless with your words. The scriptures put this truth like this:

"The tongue is a small thing, but what enormous damage it can do. A tiny spark can set a great forest on fire. And the tongue is a flame of fire. It is full of wickedness that can ruin your whole life. It can turn the entire course of your life into a blazing flame of destruction, for it is set on fire by hell itself. People can tame all kinds of animals and birds and reptiles and fish, but no

one can tame the tongue. It is an uncontrollable evil, full of deadly poison. Sometimes it praises our Lord and Father, and sometimes it breaks out into curses against those who have been made in the image of God.”** (James 3:5-9.) NLT

Notice how the text describes the effect of the words we speak to each other: Enormous damage; set on fire; blazing flame of destruction; uncontrollable evil; and full of deadly poison. In short, God is saying that this one area alone is strong enough to blow a hole the size of England in your marriage. Friends, this is serious.

Ten things you can do to reduce Unhealthy Communication.

1.) Decide To Communicate With Care.

We've already seen the havoc poor communication can inflict on a relationship. So when I say *'communicate with care'*, I mean think carefully before you say what's on your mind; because you can't take back what you've said. That's precisely why the Bible teaches us to be slow to speak.

“My dear brothers and sisters, be quick to listen, slow to speak, and slow to get angry. Your anger can never make things right in God's sight.” (James 1:19-20.) NLT

There were many times I wished I never said certain things to my wife. I wished I had remembered that she is not like me. I like people to be brutally honest with me. I feel I can take it if it is true, but my wife isn't like that at all. Each time I have tried to use my yardstick for her; I have done more damage than good. So, communicating with care is not a destination, it's a journey. I am still learning to communicate with care 25 years into our marriage.

Communicating with care means that you never shout at your spouse; you never resort to harsh or abusive language; you never wilfully dishonour or disrespect; and you never threaten to leave or divorce your partner.

> **"The intelligent person restrains his words, and one who keeps a cool head is a man of under-standing."** (Proverbs 17:27.) Holman

If you commit to communicating with that much care, your spouse will feel honoured and the conflicts you have will reduce drastically. The emotional hurts will also diminish and you'd be on your way to building the rock solid marriage you deserve.

2.) **Give Your Spouse the Gift of 'Attention'.**

Another very important thing you can do to improve your communication is to listen intently when your spouse is speaking to you. Resist the urge to butt in or cut your spouse off.
Now I know this is not easy to do, as we are often thinking of what to say next while we are still being spoken to. But you have to do this, because it is the honourable thing to do.

One strategy that may help you is to jot down the points your spouse is making while he/she is talking, so that you can respond to them one by one when it's your turn to speak.

"Understand this, my beloved brethren. Let every man be quick to hear [a ready listener], slow to speak, slow to take offences and to get angry." (James 1:19.) Amplified

When you listen attentively to what your spouse is saying:

- **You are honouring your spouse with a gift of 'attention'.**

- **You are saying that you value your spouse's opinion and concerns.**

- **You are telling your spouse that what he/she is saying is important to you.**

- **You will hear and see things that you would have missed (like body language, subliminal messages, tear drops, heart aches, cry for affirmation, etc. etc.)**

One reason why this discipline of paying attention is so crucial, is because the words we speak is believed to account for less than 20% of our intended message. The remaining 80% of the message comes from our voice tone, body language, facial expressions, and so on.

If the percentages are accurate, you could miss close to 80% of your spouse's intended message when you are not paying attention. That's why you can't continue to watch the television or be fiddling with your phone when your spouse is trying to talk to you. Courtesy demands that you switch them off.

If you train yourself to pay attention to your spouse consistently, you would not only become better at communicating, but you would even find that you become a better judge of character too. In addition, you would be well on your way to cracking the rock solid marriage puzzle.

3.) Be Open to Constructive Correction or Criticism.

Never forget that nobody is perfect. And that includes you! So, since one of the goals of your marriage is to stretch and mature you, you must be open to correction. You can't allow yourself to get so insecure and defensive that every attempt to suggest an alternative way of doing something turns into a big drama. Even if you are not sure that the suggestion or correction is ideal, learn to open up to the possibility, if it is not a life and death situation. Anything less, and pride will move in.

"First pride, then the crash— the bigger the ego, the harder the fall." (Proverbs 16:18.) Message

For instance, I am very tactile. My love language is to 'touch'. When I want to show appreciation or kindness, I put my hands on people's shoulder or around their back. I also like to be touched. So, for the first ten to fifteen years of my marriage, I didn't see anything dangerous in being this way.

Finally, my wife confronted me a few times with the dangers of my actions (especially as it pertained to the opposite sex) and I'm glad that I listened to her. I wouldn't have become more conscious of these dangers and I might have got into trouble if I wasn't willing to listen to my wives evaluation of my pet behaviour.

The point I am making is simple: Listening to your spouse's suggestions or correction or criticisms can save you from a lot of regrets and pain. You see, your spouse sees your blind-spots and loves you enough to be honest with you. Don't quench your spouse's indispensable help.

If you stay open to suggestions and corrections:

- **You will be a great example of humility to your family.**

- **Your attitude will earn you more respect from your spouse.**

- **Your partner will be able to do a better job of watching your back.**

- **You will be acknowledging that you have room in your life to continue to grow and improve. This can only be a good thing!**

4.) Try to Resolve Conflicts as Soon as Possible.

Communication is helped when conflicts and challenges in the marriage are resolved quickly. The longer things remain unresolved the more difficult it is to recall the issue accurately and objectively. The reason being that the longer a conflict simmers the more embellished it becomes in your mind.

Have you ever heard someone say, "We had a big argument, but I can't remember what it was all about."? That's because we often forget the details of the conflict, but we rarely forget the pain and the hurt it produced. Also, while the details may be hazy, our minds often intensify the feelings.

So, if it is at all possible, try to resolve misunderstandings and hurts before you go to bed. That is God's authoritative recommendation, not mine.

> **"... Don't let the sun go down while you are still angry, for anger gives a mighty foothold to the Devil.** (Ephesians 4:26-27.)

When you endeavour to resolve issues before you go to bed:

- **You are obeying God.**

- **You are destroying hazardous roots of bitterness.**

- **You are increasing your chances of sleeping soundly.**

- **You are denying Satan of a foothold in your marriage.**

5.) Learn to Share Your Feelings Without Attacking your Spouse.

This was one lesson I found really hard to master. Many times when I wanted to share my feelings with my wife, I used a 'You did this...' or 'You shouldn't have done that...' phrase. The problem with this approach is that no matter how nice you try to say it, it still sounds like an attack to your partner. It identifies your spouse as the culprit or as the one who is intentional causing your pain.

So a better way to communicate your feelings is to use 'I am feeling...' or 'It made me feel...' statements. These kinds of statements help your partner identify your feelings and concerns without igniting their defences.

If truth be told, none of us like to be accused of intentionally hurting our loved ones. But if we are faced with an unhappy spouse, we usually want to do whatever we can to turn the situation around.

So, express more of how you are feeling and less of what your spouse has or has not done. If you do, you would be helping your spouse to respond more positively to your feelings; and communication will be less stressful.

6.) **Never Humiliate or Demean Your Spouse in Public.**

It is never acceptable to humiliate your spouse in public. I don't care how angry or upset you are, you wait until you get home. You deal with your concerns in private first. If the issue is not being resolved after several attempts, I believe you should speak to a minister or marriage counsellor. But you never get into a fighting bout in a public place.

That's because it creates an impression that cannot be erased from people's minds. Even after you've resolved the issue that caused the blow-out, people are going to remember how you disgraced yourselves. Secondly, your spouse may find it extremely difficult to overlook or forgive you for such a provoking incident. Thirdly, you would be shaming the Name of the Christ you claim to represent – if you are a practising Christian.

I remember trying so hard, a few years ago, to get a husband to forgive his wife for shaming him in front of his landlord and in front of his mother-in-law. He couldn't do it. He said the pain was just too much; and after many hours of counselling, he went ahead and separated from his wife, less than three years into the marriage. Also, to show how angry he was, he threatened to expose his wife's past mistakes and apply for custody of their 18 month old child.

Husbands, you are called to love your wife to the degree that Christ loves the Church. Wives, you are called to honour and respect your husband the same way you respect Christ.[1] Well, to do that, God has not giving you any room to humiliate each other in private – talk less of in public.

7.) **Admit it When You Make Mistakes.**

Every child knows that there are three things they can do when confronted about their attitude or behaviour. They can try to deny it; they can blame something or someone else; or they can admit to it.

Denying something that is clearly your fault doesn't get you anywhere in marriage, because it doesn't resolve the issue. Blaming your spouse or somebody else is even more damaging, because it offloads your responsibility unfairly onto your partner. So the only sensible thing to do when you've blown it is to admit your failure and ask for forgiveness.

"Confess your sins to each other and pray for each other so that you may be healed. The

earnest prayer of a righteous person has great power and produces wonderful results." (James 5:16.) NLT.

Of course that begs <u>two</u> questions:

1.) **Will I do what I can to correct the situation?**

2.) **Will the forgiveness offered be genuine?**

Question one is important because just admitting to something over and over again, but not doing anything to correct it is very frustrating for your partner. Even if he/she wants to forgive and move on they can't, because it's going to happen again. It's like continually peeling the scab off an old wound; it just never heals. So you must make sure that you are doing more that just admitting to things. You must be growing, maturing, changing and correcting things that are unhealthy in your relationship.

Question two is also important because it can hinder your spouse from freely admitting their fault (or failure) to you – if they think you would hold it against them for life. Or if they think that you would use the information they give you as a weapon of shame.

Consequently, it is crucial that when you say, "I forgive you", that you really mean it; that you wipe the slate clean; and that you see any new offence as a new offence, and not as a continuation of old offences.

If you and your spouse would endeavour to follow these guidelines, you would be healthier emotionally, physically and even spiritually. Everything will be out in the open and there would be no need to allow offences to fester in the dark recesses of your mind.

8.) **Look for Ways to Build Your Spouse Up Verbally.**

We've already seen that the words we speak to each other are important. Understand that words are like containers. We use them to convey ideas, thought and requests. But words do much more than that: they impact life-changing values, graces, gifts and abilities that are far more spiritual in nature.

The Bible goes even further to tell us that the powers to give life (and to extinguish it) are invested in our words.

> **"The tongue can bring death or life; those who love to talk will reap the consequences."** (Proverbs 18:21.) NLT.

Just imagine that for a moment: You can decree death to a person or situation; or you can breathe life to that person or situation. I'll say it again because the implication of this truth is huge. **You can decree death to a person or situation; or you can breathe life to that person or situation.**

That being the case, it should be obvious that God wants you to use your words to build your partner up and not to tear him/her down. Well, how do you do that?

You build your spouse up by:

- **Being a constant Encourager to him/her.**

- **Finding and highlighting the things they do well.**

- **Affirming to him/her that they are special and loved dearly.**

- **Validating the support and effort they put into the relationship.**

- **Speaking positively and approvingly about them to outsiders.**

We live in a society that's all but starved of uplifting and encouraging experiences. The news is almost always bad. Work is almost always stressful. The economy is almost always depressed. And, life is almost always bumpy.

Therefore, make it your aim to build up your partner and to bring out the best in him/her. When you do that you are building with God. You are making a positive difference to your partner's destiny. And, you are honouring God's plan for your marriage.

If you do discipline yourself to do the above in good times and in difficult times, you will not fail to have an upbeat home and a rock solid marriage.

9.) Choose the Best Time to Settle Major Irritations.

As a couple, you must find the best time to talk things over, because talking through crucial issues will take time. You also need to make sure that you are not trying to talk when you are tired, irritable, distracted or hungry. Another unfruitful habit you must avoid when talking about important issues is multi-tasking.

I have discovered that issues of the heart require quality time and quantity attention. So seat down with your spouse and decide what time is best for you. When can you both concentrate best? When is your blood-sugar normal? Where can you seat down and talk without distraction? What needs to be switched off? And, who needs to be told not to disturb you?

This is so important that I would even encourage you to put dates in your dairy for this. If you don't, other 'urgent' things will rob you of quality time you need to smooth out your niggling anxieties.

When my children were younger, my wife and I would put them to bed, drive down to the local McDonald restaurant, buy ourselves a cup of tea (and some fries), and talk to our heart's content. As I look back over the years, those quality times apart helped to build the fabric of the marriage we enjoy today.

If you settle the little irritations in your marriage regularly, you may never need to 'call the Calvary in' to settle a major war between you and your spouse.

10.) Learn To Regularly Ask Your Spouse Whether What You Believe You Heard is what He or She Actually Meant.

I have already mentioned that the way a person communicates is a composite of upbringing, training, conditioning, personality, the situation at hand and language comprehension. None of these parts are the same for any two people.

Therefore, it's important to realise that good communication with your spouse will not happen overnight. Yes, it is complex, but you can get better at it with time.

Your spouse may hear what you said, but not interpret it the way you meant it. That's why it is always prudent to check that your spouse is on the same page with you during a serious discussion. One way to do this is to ask your spouse to repeat to you (in his/her own words) what they believe you've been saying.

Once they've done so, you will be able to correct any misunderstandings or know that your communication was successful. In the same way, when you spouse has said something important or complex to you, it is often very helpful to try to repeat what you understand his/her request to be.

If you would add this concept to your important discussions:

- **Conflicts in your marriage will reduce.**

- **You would understand each other better.**

- **Fewer misunderstandings will arise from your discussions.**

- **Your ability to communicate better would improve drastically.**

- **There would be fewer denials: "I said this" versus "No you didn't".**

Work on these ten concepts above with your spouse and you will experience God's all-sufficient grace to rise above the conflicts in your marriage. You will communicate better; understand each other better; empathise better; and live a better story. I know that is what you want, and I know that you can have it, if you want it bad enough.

"Delight yourself also in the LORD, And He shall give you the desires of your heart." (Psalm 37:4.)

---

[1] Ephesians 5:22-30.

4

STAYING TRUE TO YOUR MARRIAGE VOWS

"If a man makes a vow to the LORD, or swears an oath to bind himself by some agreement, he shall not break his word; he shall do according to all that proceeds out of his mouth." (Numbers 30:2.)

If you are planning to build a marriage that goes the distance in this marriage-dishonouring generation, you must prepare to commit 100% to the vows you say to each other on your wedding day.

The marriage vow is an eternal promise you make to your spouse and to your God in the presence of your closest friends and relations. Your vow is a covenant promise not just a legal contract. And your faithfulness and integrity is tied to it.

When you say your vows, you are promising to take good care of God's precious son or daughter. You are making an unconditional commitment to your spouse and to his or her God.

You are telling God (and everyone present) that you can be trusted to see your obligation through, irrespective of the challenges you may face. You are also declaring that you will be a man or woman of your word – as long as you have breath in you.

That's why you can't afford to take those vows lightly or dishonestly. And as a Christ-follower, it is crucial that you realise that to intentionally break your vows is to disgrace the Name of the One who saved you with His life - Jesus Christ!

> **"When you make a vow to God, do not delay to pay it; for He has no pleasure in fools. Pay what you have vowed. Better not to vow than to vow and not pay."** (Ecclesiastes 5:4-5.)

Typically, most marriage vows (but not all) consist of **four** main promises. They are:

1. **The promise to live together as husband and wife**

2. **The promise to do things God's way**

3. **The promise to love, honour and care for each other**

4. **The promise to forsake all other competing relationships**

THE PROMISE TO LIVE TOGETHER AS HUSBAND AND WIFE

In the first part of your vow, you promise to take your spouse (from that point on) to be your lawful husband or wife. From that moment on, your partner ceases to be just a boy friend or girl friend. He or she is no longer just a fiancé or fiancée.

You become husband and wife under God and under the law of the land. And, becoming husband and wife means a number of things.

In the story of creation God said, **"Therefore a man shall leave his father and mother and be joined to his wife, and they shall become one flesh."**

Then He makes this crucial observation: **"And they were both naked, the man and his wife, and were not ashamed."**[1]

The passage above teaches us a number of things about what it really means to live as husband and wife.

Firstly, it teaches that our relational priorities must change. Your spouse is now your number one priority. And only your love for God should trump this priority. You may have great parents, loving siblings or bosom friends, but they no longer have the right to take the number one spot in your life.

The text teaches that it's necessary to give up your strongest relationships for this new one with your spouse. That means that you can no longer give your best time and energy to the old relationships – no matter how precious they are to you.
Secondly, the passage above implies that couples must

intentionally cleave to each other. The Hebrew word translated 'joined' in this text carries a more graphic and permanent meaning than we are used to giving it these days. It means to 'hang on' to something as if your life depended on it.

The picture we get here is that of a climber holding tightly unto the edge of a mountain because he knows that if he lets go, he will plunge 100 metres to his death.

In other words, God wants you and your spouse to hang on to each other and unto the marriage, as if your very life depended on it. Nobody who understands this to be God's will ever takes their marriage vows lightly.

It is so sad to hear the reasons people give for getting a divorce today. I estimate that 8 out of 10 times, those marriages could have survived if the couple only took this point to heart before they decided to get married.

Thirdly, the text teaches that we must see each other as equal partners in the marriage. Becoming one flesh means more than having sex on your wedding night. Becoming one flesh is more spiritual and emotional, than physical - because people can have sex with someone they don't even like.

When the Bible uses the phrase 'one flesh', it is appealing to a deeper unity of spirit, soul and body. It is saying that couples need to see each other as partners in the same vehicle, going to the same place and both responsible for where the vehicle takes them.

So when you vow to take each other as husband and wife, you are vowing to see each other as being equally important partners in life. You are vowing to be united in purpose and to both take responsibility for where your marriage goes.

Finally, God declares that marriage is meant to be the place where we are completely open to each other. One of the drawbacks of human depravity is our tendency to hide our true identities from the people around us. We figure that if people really knew who we are and what we do, they may no longer like us.

Consequently, we go through life wearing a mask. But when you vow to take each other as husband and wife, you are making a commitment to take off the mask and be completely open to your partner.

The reasons are clear. You are now in this journey together. Both of you need to know what the deal is; what to expect; what adjustments need to be made, and so on. Well, that can't happen if things are not all laid out on the table.

I have never seen a marriage fall apart because the couple were too open and honest with each other. But I have seen marriages fall apart because one partner felt the other was closed or deceptive.

Make up your mind to cultivate a safe relationship, because openness is only possible when both of you feel safe. Being very negative or critical of your spouse destroys a safe environment. So also does abusive language, laughing at your partner and talking to others about your partner's insecurities - to mention a few.

If you want to build a rock solid marriage, you must guard against these obstacles and hindrances to sincerity, honesty and openness in your marriage. Just treat your spouse with the respect and honour with which you would wish to be treated, and chances are that you would be creating a non-threatening atmosphere conducive to openness in your home.

THE PROMISE TO DO THINGS GOD'S WAY

When you say your vows, you are also promising to live according to God's ordinance.
What is God's ordinance, as far as marriage is concerned? For the sake of brevity, I would like to distil God's ordinance into **three** crucial instructions.

i.) **Don't marry a person who is not right for you.** Not every nice looking guy or girl you meet is right for you. For instance, a person who does not share your core values or who is not willing to co-operate with your purpose or destiny is unlikely to be right for you.

"Do not be unequally yoked together with unbelievers. For what fellowship has righteousness with lawlessness? And what communion has light with darkness?" (2 Corinthians 6:14.)

ii.) **Once you've gotten married, don't try to dissolve the union because things are tough.** As a child of God, you are to commit yourself to making it work and believe that with God's help and a lot of wisdom your marriage will eventually glorify God.

"Now to the married I command, yet not I but the Lord: A wife is not to depart from her husband. But even if she does depart, let her remain unmarried or be reconciled to her husband. And a

husband is not to divorce his wife.”

(1 Corinthians 7:10-11.)

iii.) **Don't engage in any sexual activity or fantasy outside the marriage.** Why? Because all such acts defile the marriage bed, dishonour your spouse and demean the holy institution of marriage. Nobody dishonours God's institution and gets away without paying a huge price.

"Marriage is honourable among all, and the bed undefiled; but fornicators and adulterers God will judge." (Hebrews 13:4.)

That's it. The bulk of God's ordinances for married people are capture in these three instructions. If you would commit to them, you'd be well on your way to fulfilling your wedding vows and doing things God's way – instead of your way.

THE PROMISE TO LOVE, HONOUR AND CARE FOR EACH OTHER

The third promise you make to each other when you say your vows is to love, comfort, honour and keep each other until the end. This, for me, is the heart of the vows we say to each other.

<u>Love</u>: The word love in this passage is more than sex. It's much bigger than the sensual feelings we have towards each other. These are both important and needed in the relationship, but they fluctuate at the best of times.

57

The love you are promising each other here is the unconditional love that transcends good feelings. It's the God-kind of love that gives and forgives; and that is selfless and sacrificial.

It's the kind of love that never fails, because it is divinely bestowed upon us. To have this kind of love for another person though, you must first receive it.

"Behold what manner of love the Father has bestowed on us, that we should be called children of God!" (1John 3:1.)

You must know, that you know, that you are loved unconditionally by God; and know that He has deposited the same quality of love in your heart for someone else.

"...the love of God has been poured out in our hearts by the Holy Spirit who was given to us." (Romans 5:5.)

This is so important because nobody can give what they don't already possess. The moment you know that you carry divine love in your heart is the moment you know that you can love your spouse with the God-kind of love that never fails.

Do you regularly go out of your way to show unconditional love to your spouse? If you do, you would be meeting a crucial need in your spouse's life and you'd be helping to build a rock solid marriage in the process.

"Love from the centre of who you are; don't fake it." (Romans 12:10.) The Message

Comfort: When you promise to comfort each other, you are promising to be there. To be a shoulder to cry on! You are promising to spend enough time with your spouse to sooth away their pains and disappointments.

You can't sufficiently do this if you are living in different states (or countries) for extended amounts of time. You wouldn't be able to keep this promise if you refuse to talk to each other for days or weeks on end.

The point I am making is that to comfort each other, you must talk heart to heart and be sufficiently close to wrap your arms around each other as often as the need arises.

> **"Let the husband render to his wife the affection due her, and likewise also the wife to her husband."** (1 Corinthians 7:3.)

So, if you are not sufficiently tactile - if you don't like hugging or cuddling - you would need to turn this area of your life into a prayer project, because it is required to fulfil a major portion of your vows.

Although the world is teeming with people and circumstances that grieve and disquiet you along the way; God designed marriage - in part - to sooth your concerns and worries away.

When you make a point of being affectionate with your spouse - when you learn to touch, embrace, hug, kiss and caress each other daily – your emotional batteries get charged and you are able to deal courageously with whatever the world throws at you.

Do you regularly go out of your way to comfort your spouse? If you do, you would be meeting a crucial need in your spouse's life and you'd be helping to build a rock solid marriage in the process.

<u>**Honour**</u>: The next part of the traditional vow encourages us to honour each other. So, who do we usually honour? We usually honour people who we feel have done something great or have earned the right to be celebrated (e.g. Soldiers, Parents, Royalty).

When you choose to honour your spouse, you are doing several things at once.

- **You are obeying God's instructions to you in 1 Peter 3:7 and Ephesians 5:22-24 & 33.**

- **You are helping your spouse to see how highly you value and esteem him/her.**

- **You are sowing a seed that would eventually produce a harvest of honour for you.**

- **You are indirectly encouraging your spouse to rise up to the level of the honour you are ascribing to him/her.**

Let me say that again; when you honour your spouse you are encouraging your spouse to do well - to achieve, to succeed or to rise to a higher level. You are saying, "I respect you", "I see you worthy of this much honour" or "I see you coming into this much honour".

Even if you feel that your spouse does not deserve your honour yet, I want you to know that honouring your spouse in obedience to God can produce enough power to start a transformation in him/her; and improve your marriage experience altogether.

So whether you know it or not, you are creating an empowering atmosphere for the advancement of both your marriage and your life when you sincerely devote yourself to honouring your spouse. This is because, the way we treat a person often determines the way they respond to us. That is why the Bible has this to say:

"... Let the wife see that she respects and reverences her husband [that she notices him, regards him, honors him, prefers him, venerates, and esteems him; and that she defers to him, praises him, and loves and admires him exceedingly]" (Ephesians 5:33.) Amplified

"Likewise, husbands, live with your wives in an understanding way, showing honour to the woman as the weaker vessel, since they are heirs with you of the grace of life, so that your prayers may not be hindered." (1 Peter 3:7.) ESV.

Do you make a point of honouring your spouse? If you do, you would be meeting an important need in your spouse's life and you'd be helping to make sure that your prayers are not hindered.

Keep: To 'keep' your spouse means to 'look after' your spouse. When you say your vows, you are promising to take special care of your partner irrespective of what is going on in your lives.

In too many relationships, the lack of care and consideration becomes the root of bitterness that eventually kills the marriage. Don't let this happen to you. Remember that you promised to care for your spouse in sickness and in health, whether you are rich or poor, or whether things are good or bad.

One of the joys of my marriage, is knowing that my wife sees it as her responsibility to look after me as best as she can, and I know that it is my responsibility to look after her no matter what we are going through.

For instance, there were times I upset my wife and fully expected her to show me to the kitchen when I got hungry. But it never happened. She would always cook for me, serve me and call me to the table even when she was still upset with me.

Why? Because that's what we promised each other when we took our vows 25 years ago. But we didn't just make this promise to each other; we made it to God in the presence of over two hundred people.

I was so impressed by my wife's response to me one day that I asked her why she always maintained a caring attitude towards me even when she was upset about something I had done. She told me that her Mother warned her before she got married never to starve her husband under any circumstance. Thank God for wise Mothers too!

"Don't look out only for your own interests, but take an interest in others, too." (Philippians 2:4.) NLT

If you remind yourself regularly that your marriage vows were as much to God as they were to your spouse, and if you respect and revere God like you should, you will always seek to keep your vow irrespective of the challenges of marriage life.

You would also take delight in caring for your spouse because you promised to do so and because that's the only tangible way you can prove to your spouse that you really love him/her.

THE PROMISE TO FORSAKE
ALL OTHERS

In the last part of the marriage vows, you promised to treat your spouse in an exclusive and special manner.

You promised to respectfully exclude all other 'contenders' and everyone who feel that they should have a stake in your marriage. And, you promised to stay faithful to your spouse till the end comes for either or both of you

Now this vow is not saying that you can't have any friends, acquaintances or relatives. But it does imply that your relationship with them can no longer be in the same league as the one you have with your spouse. Those relationships must all be put in a distant forth, fifth or sixth place.

I like to put it like this: For every hour you are willing to spend with a friend, you must be willing to spend ten or more hours with your spouse. For every pound you are willing to spend on your extended family, you must be prepared to spend a hundred pounds on your spouse (and children when they arrive).

For every time you forgive a colleague for offending you, you must be ready to forgive your spouse a hundred times. Why? **Because you made a promise to do so when you vowed to exalt your relationship with your spouse above every other human relation-ship.**

Now I know that many traditions and cultures of the world

encourage couples to change this priority. They say things like, "You only have one mother or father, but you can always get another wife or husband".

Or they say, "Blood is thicker than water" - meaning that your family is 'blood' and your spouse is like 'water'. Or they say, 'Family is forever' - implying that your marriage is dispens-able.

As practical as these world-views may sound to the untrained ear, they are not rooted in the wisdom of God. If you open yourself up to these humanistic views, you are not only courting legitimate jealously and discontentment in your marriage, but you are disconnecting yourself from the grace and help that God gives to all who obey His word and heed His wisdom.

By the way, your spouse is bone of your bones, and flesh of your flesh. The last time I looked, bone and flesh was thicker than blood.

In the final analysis, God instituted marriage and knows what makes it work perfectly. And He said, "For this reason a man shall leave his father and mother and be joined to his wife, and the two shall become one flesh."

The point of this chapter is to help you see that your marriage vows are not just nice words you say to impress the crowd, but covenant promises that you make to your spouse and to his or her God.

Consequently, God expects you to bend over backwards to keep them. The good news is that He has made a way for you by promising to actually help you keep your vows, if you would put your trust and faith in Him.

"Fear not, for I am with you; be not dismayed, for

I am your God. I will strengthen you, yes, I will help you, I will uphold you with My righteous right hand." (Isaiah 41:10.)

I challenge you to believe this promise; because if you do, you will find grace and strength to keep every one of your vows, even when things are tough in the marriage. I know this for a fact, because I have been there.

[1] Genesis 2:24-25.

5

MEETING YOUR SPOUSE'S DEEPEST NEEDS

The husband should give to his wife her conjugal rights, and likewise the wife to her husband. For the wife does not rule over her own body, but the husband does; likewise the husband does not rule over his own body, but the wife does.

(1 Corinthians 7:3-4.)

As you embark on your marital journey, understand that you are in a divine institution that thrives on sacrifice and suffocates wherever selfishness reigns. In other words, marriage does not work well for self-centred or self-absorbed people.

For instance, Charlton and Sheila had only been married for a year when Sheila confided in a friend that she was considering separating from her husband.

When her friend asked why she wanted to go down that path so soon after their twenty thousand dollar wedding, she replied that her husband didn't really love her.

"Why do you feel this way", her friend quizzed.

"Charlton doesn't care about me. He buys whatever he needs for himself, whether we can afford it or not; but if I want something he does his best to prove to me that I don't need it - or that I can do without it."

"He goes out to see his friends three to four times a week, but expects me to stay home everyday. He even sends large sums of money to help his siblings abroad, but didn't want me to buy a Christmas gift for my mother last year."

What was the problem in this marriage? Blatant selfishness! Charlton failed to identify or meet his wife's perceived needs. And what was the result? **Feelings of dissatisfaction, disappointment and legitimate jealousy.**

You see, when you fail to identify and lovingly meet the needs of your spouse, you open the door to trouble. This is because we all go into the marital relationship to meet some of our deeply seated needs for love, affection, companionship, children, security and sexual fulfilment - to mention a few.

When any of these needs are left unmet (intentionally or otherwise) we feel incomplete, at best, or we experience a deep sense of betrayal. That's why the Bible teaches: "Let the husband render to his wife the affection due her, and likewise also the wife to her husband."[1]

Now I am aware that there are some needs that nobody but God can meet in your life. I am not referring to these needs. I am talking about those legitimate needs that husbands expect their wives to meet, and those that wives have a right to expect from their husbands.

So if you want to build the kind of marriage that would stand the test of time and conflict, you need to make it your duty to find out what your spouse's top needs are and you need to focus seriously on finding creative ways to meet them.

"We then who are strong ought to bear with the scruples of the weak, and not to please ourselves."
(Romans 15:1.)

The Conclusions Of Many Marital Surveys

Scores of surveys have been carried out on men and women over the past six decades or so to find out what our deeply felt needs are. Without boring you with pages of statistical information, and before we look at the most popularly expressed needs of men and women, here is a summary of the most relevant conclusions to these surveys:

1.) That both men and women enter the marriage relationship with several distinct needs: Physical, Emotional, Financial, Sexual, Spiritual, etc. etc.

2.) That the perceived needs of men and women are distinctly different; or are usually prioritised differently even when they are similar.

3.) That when couples discover and carefully endeavour to meet each other's needs, their relationships are stronger and they are happier together.

4.) That when these needs are not intentionally identified and met, the marriage is more volatile, and couples are proportionally more unstable and unhappy.

Men's Needs Versus Women's Needs

In the book 'His Needs, Her Needs', Author and Marriage Counsellor, Willard F. Harley, shares what his research has shown to be the top five needs of men and the top five needs of women - mainly across North America.

Harley lists these needs in order of importance. Men's top five most basic needs are:

1. **Sexual Fulfilment**
2. **A Recreational Companion**
3. **An Attractive Spouse**
4. **Domestic Support**
5. **Admiration**

Women's top five basic needs are:

1. **Affection**
2. **Conversation**
3. **Honesty & Openness**
4. **Financial Support**
5. **Family Commitment**

Harley admits that the lists above is not absolute for all men or women, but feels that they are fairly accurate for most couples in his surveys. My point is not to debate the accuracy of the lists above, but to show you that men and women do enter into marriage with distinct needs and that those needs are usually totally different.

That being the case, the couple that wants to build a rock solid marriage, must endeavour to find out what their partners list of needs are. In my opinion, the best way to find out is to ask.

If you are not sure of what your spouse might consider to be the basic needs he/she would like you to meet, there is no shame in asking. Your spouse is more likely to appreciate the fact that you cared to ask. But if you ask, be prepared to follow through. If you can't fulfil some needs for a time, be open enough to let your spouse know why.

Learning from Ade and Bev

Ade and Bev had only been married for six months when they were invited to a Marriage Workshop – where the topic of this chapter was to be discussed. They both agreed after the event that they hadn't been meeting each other's basic needs and were determined to put things right.

The first thing they did when they got home from the day-long workshop was to spend the evening talking about what they both expected from the marriage. They then came up with a list of their top six basic needs and talked about what they would do to meet those needs for each other.

One of Ade's top needs was to make passionate love to his wife every morning before he went to work. Although Bev was willing to agree to this if it would make her husband happy, she explained how it would make her tired and often late for the first part of her Masters programme. She also explained that she didn't want to have sex on certain days in the month because she didn't want to get pregnant until she was nearing the end of her course. Finally, she reassured her husband that she was committed to meeting his needs, but asked for his understanding on the issues she had raised.

Ade felt he understood his wife better for the first time since they got married. They agreed on a compromise and their sexual life became more meaningful and less stressful.

Also, one of Bev's top basic needs was for more affirmation and affection. Bev wanted Ade to be more romantic and to affirm her more - instead of his usual critical and biting remarks to her. Ade explained that he was following in his father's footsteps and didn't really know any better. He also apologised for treating his wife the way his father treated his mother.

Finally, Ade asked Bev to help him change by blowing him a kiss (as a signal) any time he starts to slip back into his former behaviour. Many years later, Ade and Bev insist that the decisions they took on that faithful day saved their marriage.

WHY YOU MUST DECIDE TO MEET YOUR SPOUSE'S NEEDS

There are several reasons why you must commit yourself to meeting your spouse's basic needs:

1. **It is the conjugal duty you owe to your spouse**

   When you spoke your marriage vows, you where promising to take on certain responsibilities in the marriage. One of those responsibilities includes fulfilling some of your spouse's needs that nobody else is meant to meet. Yes, it would require sacrifice, but if you take delight in meeting those needs, you cannot fail to build a rock solid marriage.

2. **It is the evidence that you really love your spouse**

Love is a verb. It is an action word. You can't really say you love somebody and not think of making them happy. Well, your spouse can't be totally happy and fulfilled if their basic needs stay unmet for long periods of time. So, every deliberate effort to meet your spouse's basic needs is proof that you really love him/her.

3. **It is the pattern your children will see and emulate**

Psychologists and sociologist are right to remind us that up to 80% of our children's attitude and behaviour come directly from what they observe and learn in the home. They also tell us that the chances of turning out just like our parents are alarmingly high. That said, there is no better example that you can set for your children than to genuinely express tonnes of kindness and consideration to your spouse in front of them.

4. **It is the confirmation that you are a person of integrity**

Integrity is never easy to maintain. Life and circumstances often conspire to make you drop your standards. Yes, you made a promise, but you don't think your partner is living up to their part of the bargain - you figure. But integrity has nothing to do with what somebody else does or doesn't do. Integrity has to do with you. So when you promise to meet your spouse's need for respect, or honesty, or openness, or financial support, or sex – you do it because your reputation is on the line. You draw on God grace and fulfil your pledge. That's what a man or woman of integrity does, even if they have to do it on 'credit'.

5. **It is the proof that you are grateful to God for His Priceless Gift to you**

Lastly, your determination to meet your spouse's basic needs is proof that you value the 'priceless gift of a spouse' that God has given to you. No, your spouse is not perfect. Your partner may not even be all you had hope for. But at least you have a partner. That makes you more blessed than millions of people in our world who go to their graves lonely and alone every year.

Also, the object of marriage is not to start with a perfect partner, but to end with one, as you sharpen and build each other. In short, your marriage is often the tool God uses to mature and perfect you and your spouse. So, be grateful for the 'gift' you have, because that's what will motivate you to keep pressing on when times are tough.

Conclusion:

As I conclude my thoughts on this chapter, I want to add that our needs generally change over time. Even when they don't completely change, our order of priority often does. For instance, your basic needs may change when a child is born, or when the child starts school, or even when all your children have left home. As my wife and I have gotten older, we've noticed a shift in the intensity and order of our basic needs.

When that happens in your relationship, I encourage you to talk about it again and (if necessary) reorganise your life to meet the new needs. At each point sacrifice, flexibility, commitment and understanding will be required from the two of you, but the result can be magical.

In addition, you would have learnt to serve your spouse in a way that uplifts him/her and in a way that pleases the Lord. God is not unjust to overlook such a sacrifice and He promises to reward you for honouring His instructions.

"For God is not unjust to forget your work and labour of love which you have shown toward His name, as you minister to others..." (Hebrew 6:10.)

If you would get enthusiastic about intentionally meeting your spouse's needs, your spouse would have no choice but to reciprocate if he/she has a conscience. But more importantly, you would have the satisfaction of knowing that you honoured God and did what was right in His sight. That kind of satisfaction is 'worth its weight in gold'.

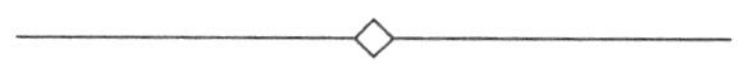

[1] 1 Corinthians 7:3.

6

ADJUSTING TO YOUR PARTNER'S UNIQUENESS

You made all the delicate, inner parts of my body and knit me together in my mother's womb. Thank you for making me so wonderfully complex! Your workmanship is marvellous – and how well I know it. (Psalm 139:13-14.) NLT

If you want to have a great marriage, you must realise that it has to be built on a commitment to give and give. Yes, I do mean give and give. Give love; give honour; give affection; give forgiveness; give support; and give plenty of encouragement.

When I was a young man, I heard people say, "Marriage is give and take". And I understand what they were trying to say. But when I was struggling to build the marriage I had always hoped for, I heard an inner voice say, "The secret is to keep on giving".

"Give, and it will be given to you: good measure, pressed down, shaken together, and running over will be put into your bosom. For with the same

measure that you use, it will be measured back to you." (Luke 6:38.)

In most Churches you will only hear preachers talk about this verse when they are trying to take up a free will offering. But the context of this Bible truth has little to do with money. Jesus was teaching his disciples to keep giving love, and forgiveness, and mercy, and consideration, and charity. The point He was making is that His disciples (which should include you, if you call yourself a Christian) were to focus on the 'giving' side of the equation.

You see, no marriage can last very long if the couple involved are constantly 'taking' stuff from each other; if they are making huge emotional and physical withdrawals from the marriage, but are putting very little back into it. Eventually, your physical or emotional love-bank runs dry. But if you and your spouse are more eager to 'give' than to 'take', your love bank-balance will always be plentiful.

Years ago, I read a book that helped me understand this concept extremely well. The author explained that when any two people meet each other and decide to develop a friendship, they start out with an empty love-account for each other.

Say, the guy does something incredibly sweet and caring for the girl, he inadvertently increases the balance of his love-account in her heart. The more he cares and gives her what she needs, the larger his account balance grows in her heart. You could say 'love-units' are being deposited into his love-account in her heart.

Similarly, if the guy behaves like a blockhead and hurts her feelings, his love units in her heart decreases to the degree that he has hurt her.

Every time the girl responds in a positive, respectful and loving way to the guy, a deposit of love-units are made into his love-bank; and her love-units in his heart increase accordingly.

The writer went on to explain that this deposit and withdrawal keeps on happening between the couple until they feel that they either can't stand each other or can't live without each other.

Those who feel that they can't or don't want to live without each other typically decide to get married; and those who don't, go their separate ways.

What really challenged me about this concept is what the writer said next. He said that most couples work doubly hard to deposit the maximum number of love-units into their spouse's heart while courting, but often fail to continue doing so after they get married. What a tragedy!

He concluded that most couples would not inflict as much pain on each other if they only spent a fraction of the time and energy they spent making deposits into their partner (after the marriage) as they spent before they walked down the aisle.

The point I am making is this. If you find yourself adapting and adjusting to your partner during your courtship, you are going to need to double up your effort when you are married.

Your spouse is going to do a number of things differently. And when that happens I want you to ask yourself these questions:

- **Is this worth fighting over?**
- **Is this a major issue that needs to be addressed**

now?

- **Is this issue a non-negotiable deal?**

- **Is there a way to solve this issue so that both of us win?**

- **How can I respond to this situation in such a way that I make a deposit instead of a withdrawal?**

No two human beings are exactly the same, so I can guarantee that your spouse is going to differ from you in many ways. Some of the differences may be very complimentary and you may be pleased that you have a spouse who compliments you in those particular ways.

However, a number of those differences may worry and bug you. The trick is to understand that it is okay for your spouse to be different; and to know how to adapt and adjust without losing your individuality and without inflicting unnecessary damage on your spouse.

Of course, I am not referring here to blatantly negative or immoral behaviour - like lying, or stealing, or hitting, or flirting with the opposite sex. You should never adjust to these. Get help! Talk to someone who can intervene before it's too late. These fall into the 'non-negotiable' category.

I am referring here to differences in taste, or choices, or methods, or even personality traits.

Lessons from Toby and Margaret

For instance, 26 year old, Margaret has always been quiet and a bit shy. But when she met Toby, she fell head over heels in love with him. Toby was everything that Margaret wasn't. And that was partly why she was attracted to him.

They got married a year later with hopes of a blissful future. Two and a half years into their marriage, Toby confided in his House Group that he wished he had married someone more like himself.

He complained that his wife didn't like going out with him; and when she did venture out she preferred to sit quietly in the corner of the room. She never seems to have an opinion about anything; and she didn't want him to throw her a 30th birthday party.

Finally, he bleated out in exasperation, "I think marrying an introvert was a big mistake."

Now I don't think Toby's problem is really his wife's temperament, but his desire to make her into his image. And that never works in a marriage. God often brings opposites together so that both can contribute what makes them unique to the union.

Of course, it would be helpful if Margaret could move a little towards meeting her husband's need for companionship and fun. That's what people who love each other do. They stretch beyond their comfort to meet their partner's need because they love their partner. But marrying an introvert was not the mistake here. The mistake in this marriage was not adapting; not adjusting; not being patient; and not appreciating the personality traits of the other person.

"Love each other with genuine affection, and take delight in honouring each other." (Romans 12:10.)

In talking to couples, I am never surprised when I find out that one of the main sources of conflict in the relationship has to do with the different ways the couple each respond to life issues or the way they have learnt to process things.

Thus, if the couple see something in their marriage as a problem to be solved and it doesn't get solved, they believe that they have a problem that can't be solved. If, on the other hand, they view that same issue as a stepping stone to greater intimacy and refuse to give up until they achieve that intimacy, they generally do.

Lessons from John and Valerie

John grew up in a very strict home. His father was a decorated captain in the British Army and often raved about the lack of discipline and order amongst young people. So he ran his home like a military boot camp.

John met Valerie in a friend's party and was attracted to her carefree and tactile personality. Not only was she the proverbial 'life of the party', but she made him feel special and masculine by flirting with him all through the evening.

Five years into their marriage, and after having two children together, John can't stand Valerie. Why? Because she talks too much, has too many friends and is not as disciplined with the house chores and the children, as he wants her to be.

What is John's real problem? He has forgotten why he was so attracted to her in the first place. He has not cared to factor her upbringing or her personality into his expectations. And, he is unfairly comparing his upbringing with that of his children who are growing up under different circumstances and in a totally different era.

John believes his strict upbringing is superior to Valerie's and should be the way his children are brought up. In short, he wants her to do things his way. He wants to make her into his image and likeness.

Let me say it again, this strategy never works – except you have an insecure spouse who doesn't mind being trampled over. And even then, one day your spouse would explode if that strategy is not discarded soon.

If truth be told, most people don't do well trying to live as somebody else.

Why God made us all Unique

Men and women are very different, but in a complimentary way. The way a man and a woman interlock sexually is a vivid image of how they are designed to interconnect psychologically, emotionally and even spiritually.

These differences should not be barriers to a fulfilling relationship, but incentives to explore and grow with your partner more fully. By that I mean, your partner's differences are there to make him/her continuously intriguing and fascinating to you – so you never get bored with each other.

The differences between you are there:

- **To keep you fascinated and interested in each other.**

- **To keep you learning and discovering more about each other.**

- **To help you develop a selfless and sacrificial attitude towards each other.**

- **To help you explore and appreciate each other's unique qualities and virtues.**

- **To help you grow and mature as you learn to understand and adjust to each other.**

Once you start to see your differences in this light, you will never again see your differences as a negative thing. Instead, you would see your differences as life's way of stretching, maturing and polishing you in certain areas of your life.

You'll also view your differences as God's way of helping you to learn how to enjoy life outside of your comfort zone. You'll see your differences as God's way of purging you of pride and selfishness, and helping you to develop a sacrificial attitude – as you learn to embrace and love a very different personality from yours.

> **"Let nothing be done through selfish ambition or conceit, but in lowliness of mind let each esteem others better than himself."** (Philippians 2:3.)

For example, in most relationships, you would find that couples have traits that are generally opposite in nature. The man may be fun-loving and out-going, while his wife may be very reserved. The woman may be well-organized and disciplined while her husband may be untidy, sloppy or carefree.

The man may be a big spender, while his wife is big on saving her money. My point is, neither spending nor saving is wrong, but for this relationship to blossom in the area of their finances like it should, the couple are going to have to learn to adapt a philosophy of finances that is somewhere in the middle.

That's going to take understanding, humility, maturity, sacrifice and even compromise on occasions. But, it is precisely this kind of dilemma in our marriages that God uses to stretch and transforms us, if we follow His instructions.

God's Instructions

Our heavenly Father loves us so much that He bent over backwards to put instructions into our hands. And, His instructions are pretty simple. But you must be ready to embrace them and do them.

It's doing what God instructs couples to do that produces the results. So here are a few of those simple instructions. Read them and ask yourself whether you are prepared to obey them in your marriage.

"Let nothing be done through selfish ambition or conceit, but in lowliness of mind let each esteem others <u>better</u> than himself." (Philippians 2:3.)

"Be kindly affectionate to one another with brotherly love, in honour giving <u>preference</u> to one another..." (Romans 12:10.)

"...Yes, all of you be <u>submissive</u> to one another, and be clothed with humility, because "God resists the

proud, But gives grace to the humble."

(1 Peter 5:5b.)

"But if you are bitterly jealous and there is selfish ambition in your hearts, don't brag about being wise. That is the worst kind of lie. For jealousy and selfishness are not God's kind of wisdom. Such things are earthly, unspiritual, and motivated by the Devil. For wherever there is jealousy and selfish ambition, there you will find disorder and every kind of evil. But the wisdom that comes from heaven is first of all pure. It is also peace loving, gentle at all times, and <u>willing</u> <u>to</u> <u>yield</u> to others. It is full of mercy and good deeds. It shows no partiality and is always sincere." (James 3:14-17.) NLT.

Notice the words underlined above. Do they represent the general attitude in your home? Do you esteem your spouse better than yourself in some areas? Do you prefer to go with your spouse's ideas in those areas? Do you submit to some of your spouse's suggestions, or do all the suggestions have to come from you? Are you willing to yield to your spouse, or are you always trying to change him/her?

Do yourself and your spouse a big favour and understand:

- That your spouse has as much right as you to be unique and different.

- That the differences between you are not obstacles, but stepping stones to a richer marriage life.

- That your differences do not have to divide and frustrate you, if you embrace the purpose for them.

- That God uses the differences between you and your spouse to stretch and mature you for a higher assignment.

Allowing your spouse to be the unique person God has created him/her to be is a sure sign of your maturity in that area. But even more impressive, is your ability to celebrate your spouse's uniqueness in private and in public. If you will do this from your heart, you will cut years of conflict and frustration from your marriage life. And your spouse would, more than likely, reciprocate the affirming gesture.

7

KEEPING GOD AT THE CENTRE OF YOUR MARRIAGE

"Three cords twisted together are not easily broken."
(Ecclesiastes 4:12b.) BBE

Most people you talk to would define marriage as a union between a man and a woman. And although there is body of truth in this definition, it is not a technically accurate definition for enlightened Christians.

Biblically, marriage is between a man, a woman and the God who brought them together. Marriage can never be as strong as it was designed to be if God is not seen as an integral part of the union.

In fact, God is the only constant in the relationship. The man may change; the lady may change; their circumstances may change; but God stays immutable and unchangeable.

It was this threefold union that the ancient King was referring to when he said, "Three cords twisted together cannot be easily broken." Solomon was saying that marriages would not fall apart so readily if God is seen and honoured as the third and most significant partner in it.

Consequently, if you want to build a rock solid marriage in this marriage-dishonouring generation, you must commit to keeping God at the centre of your marriage upfront. That's the real starting point; and things never really come together like they should for the Christian couple who have not made this crucial and foremost commitment.

Keeping God at the centre of your marriage implies a number of things:

- It implies that you will need to wholeheartedly embrace God's leadership in your home and in your dealings with your partner at all times.

- It implies that you will not make any important decisions or take any important steps, without running it through the plumb line of God's will for your marriage.

- It implies that you would choose to pray and study God's Word together; and commit yourselves to obeying what it teaches at every turn.

- It implies that you would respect, honour and treat your spouse just as you would if Jesus Christ (personally) lived in your home and went everywhere with you in the marriage.

In short, keeping God at the centre of your marriage is hard work. It can't be done with a nonchalant attitude and you wouldn't succeed unless you have a strong desire to honour God completely in your life and marriage.

Six Things You Can Do To Keep God At The Centre Of Your Marriage

1.) Find time to study the Bible and pray with your spouse at least two or three times a week.

We live in a world that crowds our time with so many 'urgent' things, that we often forget to do the important things. Praying and studying the Bible together is one of those important things that often suffer in marriage, if care is not taken. But the spiritual health of your marriage depends on it.

So finding time to keep your divine connection intact is crucial. In fact, I will not be exaggerating to say that praying and studying together is the one thing you can't ignore if you want God to continue to speak to you and if your want His influence to be central in your marriage.

"Then you will call upon Me and go and pray to Me, and I will listen to you. And you will seek Me and find Me, when you search for Me with all your heart." (Jeremiah 29:12-13.)

So, if God is to remain at the centre of your marriage, He will need to instruct you and your spouse regularly. Studying the Bible and praying together is the most common way He does that.

Schedule it if you must, but make sure that you do it, because your spiritual health really depends on it.

2.) Schedule time to read inspirational books, listen to motivational talks, and watch uplifting films or programmes together.

Most of us are bombarded daily with discouraging and de-motivating challenges. Whether it's from the morning news, the horrendous traffic, the incorrigible colleague at work or the numerous setbacks of life, the outcome is the same: deflation, despondency, despair or even depression.

So there's probably no better way to keep yourself and your marriage refreshed than making time to read together, listen to something inspirational together, or watch something positive together.

The things you feed your mind and spirit on, is going to determine what priorities you embrace. So, if your priority is to keep God in the centre of your marriage, you will need to consume and focus more on spiritually uplifting 'soul-food'.

> **"Finally, brethren, whatever things are true, whatever things are noble, whatever things are just, whatever things are pure, whatever things are lovely, whatever things are of good report, if there is any virtue and if there is anything praiseworthy--meditate on these things."**
>
> (Philippians 4:8.)

3.) Find a great Church and together with your spouse commit to be a diligent, contributing couple (or family) there.

If you want your home to be a God-honouring home, you must honour God's instructions to stay connected to other like-minded Christians. The Christian faith was not designed to be lived in isolation, but in fellowship with others.

"And let us consider one another in order to stir up love and good works, not forsaking the assembling of ourselves together, as is the manner of some, but exhorting one another, and so much the more as you see the Day approaching." (Hebrews 10:24-25.)

God designed the local Church to be a place where you can go to connect with a growing spiritual family. God knew that you would need such a family, where you can receive encouragement, support and instruction; and where you can also use your time, talents and treasure to serve Him and His people.

Furthermore, God designed the Church to provide you with an indispensable support system; as the leaders and members of the Church model for you how the Christian life is meant to be lived.

In addition, every time you make a meaningful contribution to the local Church, you are setting into motion the Law of Reciprocals (also called the Law of Sowing and Reaping). And, you need to know that your sowing will eventually attract a timely reward for you.

"Those who sow in tears shall reap in joy."

(Psalms 126:5.)

If you would commit to a good local Church because you understand and embrace the truth above, you will not only experience more opportunities for spiritual growth and maturity, but find that the Church will aid you in your commitment to keep God at the centre of their marriage.

4.) **Pepper your home with striking artefacts, plaques, posters, pictures, or drawings that remind you of God's vital partnership in your marriage.**

Out of sight, they say, is out of mind. That's why we often forget important things that should never be forgotten. That's also why we write a list of things we want to do or buy.

So the idea here is to intentionally place things all around you that would continually remind you to keep God at the centre of your marriage. Whether it's a painting, a drawing, a picture or an artefact, is not that important. What is important is that it jogs your memory and focuses your energies in the right direction.

> **"And these words which I command you today shall be in your heart... "You shall bind them as a sign on your hand, and they shall be as frontlets between your eyes. "You shall write them on the doorposts of your house and on your gates."** (Deuteronomy 6:6,8,9.)

For example, a few years ago, my wife told me that something I inadvertently did often, upset her. After she discussed the issue with me for the fourth or fifth time, I realised that I was repeating the same behaviour because I kept forgetting how it made her feel.

So I put a note in my Bible to remind me about this issue

everyday as I opened it to study. Sure enough, I soon stopped offending my wife in this way. Why? Because, I was reminded about the issue regularly for weeks – until it became second nature.

God instructed His people to put signs, tablets and plaques around their homes to remind them of His commandments because He knows how forgetful we can be.

Peppering your home, office or vehicle with reminders of what you are trying to achieve can help you keep God at the centre of your marriage. If it works for you, you would be wise to use it.

5.) Keep and nurture friends who are striving to go where you want to go, or who have already got there in their relationships.

"Evil company", they say, "corrupts good manners"[1]. But the converse is also true. That's why it is important to watch the friends and friendships we keep. Human beings are generally highly influenced by the crowd we move with. The Ancient text expresses this truth well when it says:

"The righteous should choose his friends carefully, because the way of the wicked leads them astray." (Proverbs 12:26.)

If you really want to honour God and keep Him at the centre of your marriage, you must find people who are best suited to help you stay on course. You must be willing to invest in them in any way you can, so that they may in turn be motivated to invest in you.

When my children were very young, I often wished that some of the younger couples or single people in our Church would help us look after them for a few hours. As it happened, too many of them seemed too busy to help us at the time.

If they had helped us at the time, my wife and I would have been thrilled to bless those young people with so much more than money. We would have shared our experiences and showered our prayers on them. And, just maybe, the grace that is upon our marriage, may have robbed off on theirs too.

A wise counsellor once said, "Show me your friends and I will show you your future". What he meant was that your friends and acquaintances will influence your destiny. If that is true (and I'm positive it is) you must choose them carefully.

6.) **Practice the presence of God daily.**

The phase 'practicing the presence of God' has been used for years in Christendom to describe the intentional act of worshiping, praying, or meditating about God in order to connect with Him in a more personal and tangible way.

After all, God promised to reveal Himself to us when we take Him seriously.

> **"Then you will seek Me, inquire for, and require Me [as a vital necessity] and find Me when you search for Me with all your heart."** (Jeremiah 29:13.) Amplified

When you seek God in this way sincerely, you can expect to

sense God's powerful presence, hear His convicting voice or experience His overwhelming peace regularly. The Bible is full of people who experienced these acts of God while they were praying or fasting or worshipping.

So, whether you are cooking, cleaning, ironing, clearing the yard or making love; endeavour to remember that you are in the presence of God. That God is Omnipresent. That He is everywhere. The more you keep that truth on your mind, the more God's tangible presence will become real to you.

It's similar to the phenomenon that happens when you decide to buy a particular kind of car or shoe or handbag. You immediately start to see that particular type of car or shoe or handbag everywhere you go. Now, those cars and shoes and handbags were always around you, but because you had little or no interest in them earlier on, they did not attract your attention so much.

Well, when you decide to focus your attention and thoughts on the presence of God, you will start to experience more of His presence. You will become more conscious and aware that the Almighty God is indeed with you. And, your relationship with your spouse will reflect that new awareness.

Your desire to keep God at the centre of your marriage will become easier as you become more conscious of His tangible presence in your home and life. That's what practicing the presence of God will do for you.

[1] 1 Corinthians 15:33.

8

CARING PASSIONATELY
FOR EACH OTHER

"Love from the centre of who you are; don't fake it."
(Romans 12:10.) The Message

Marriage is not for sissies or promise breakers. But it works marvellously for couples who have learnt to be caring, selfless and generous with each other. Marriage is the one institution that separates the 'men' from the 'boys' – so to speak. It is the one endeavour that calls for true humility, maturity, sacrifice and tenacity.

Don't expect anything less from your marriage, because it was designed to give you a taste of heaven on earth, if you get it right. But from all that we've discussed, it should be obvious by now that we can't do marriage without genuine love for each other.

The kind of love that works in the marriage institution is the type that never fails: the type that is truly kind, patient, considerate, sacrificial, and humble. It's the love that comes from God himself.

The Apostle Paul tells us that this kind of unquenchable love has been deposited in our hearts. That means that you already have this love in you. You can love totally. You can be kind. You can be considerate. You can care. You can be patient with your spouse. It's all within your reach and your power.

So never again say, "I can't do this". Never utter the words, "I don't love him/her any more". That's a lie from the pit of hell. You can and you will, if you believe God's Word to be true. And, He says that:

- **He will supply everything you need[1]**

- **You are more than a conqueror in Christ[2]**

- **You are equipped with His love for the task[3]**

- **You can have the desires of your heart[4]**

- **You can do all things through Christ who strengthens you[5]**

It's true that we live in a season when marriage is minimised, devalued, trivialised and even scorned in some quarters. Nevertheless, a marriage based on God's precepts can be a shining light in a dark world.

Consequently, this is a challenge to really care for your spouse. It is a call to defy the statistics and the 'Nay-Sayers'. It is a challenge to be different and to allow the grace of God in you to shine for the world to see. Because, when you really love and care for your spouse:

- **You are fulfilling your marriage vows**

- **You are taking care of the 'gift' God gave you**

- **You are setting a standard for future generations**

- **You are making yourself qualified for more of God's blessings**

- **You are sweetening the life of a precious man or woman; and**

- **You are proving the devil to be a liar and God's Word to be true.**

It's a win-win for both of you and for all those who look up to you.

Take the Initiative

There is one more thought I would like to leave with you if your marriage has been going through a real bad patch. I want you to make up your mind to be the key person God would use to change things. When couples are facing challenging situations, they each wait for the other one to make the move towards resolution or reconciliation.

But I want to challenge you to be the person who initiates reconciliation because you have read this book. Even if you think your spouse is at fault, all that matters is that the issue gets resolved. **So be the bigger person**. Be the one who raises the white flag whenever there is conflict. Be the one God can depend on to do the right thing in your marriage.

Don't be afraid that your spouse would take advantage of you, if you make the first move. Know that doing the right thing for your marriage is more important than counting the scores. If you are the one calling on God to save your marriage, you are the one who would have to make the biggest sacrifices to change the atmosphere. You are the one who should 'bell the cat'.

Somebody Needs To Bell the Cat?

I'll never forget the first time I heard the story of the mice and the annoying cat. The cat was the villain because he was killing the mice off one by one when they least expected. So, one day, the mice community had a meeting to decide how best to nullify the threat to their survival and save their ever shrinking population.

After hours of heated discussion, one mouse suggested that the best solution would be to place a bell around the cat's neck, so that the cat would no longer be able to sneak up on them by surprise.

"Great idea", everyone thought.

"But who would bell the cat?" asked another mouse. "Who amongst us would risk his life to put a huge ringing bell around the cat's neck?" As you can imagine, there was a deafening silence.

Although I was no more than seven years old when I first heard this story, the moral of the story has stuck with me all these years. **It is one to thing come up with a great idea or plan, but it is quite another thing to actually execute it.**

The point I make here is simply that, it is never easy to take responsibility for changing an undesirable situation. There is no guarantee that the action you take will work; and like the mice and cat story, you may even endanger yourself in the process.

Fortunately, when it comes to relationships, the outcome is not always as bleak. No matter how tough things may have been in your marriage recently, you no doubt were deeply in love with each other at one time. Well, that means it can happen again for you. There is hope!

Secondly, your spouse probably wants things in the marriage to change too. I can't imagine that anyone in their right mind likes a turbulent or joyless marriage. My guess is that your spouse wants things to change, but does not know what to do or where to start from. Sometimes the problem is pride, or fear, or hurts, or ignorance. But if there is a desire for things to change, there is hope.

Thirdly, if you put your trust and faith in God, there is always hope! Hope that things will change. Hope that the things you have learnt will work. Hope that your spouse will work with you to build a rock solid marriage. In fact, the Scriptures teach us that because Christ is living in us, He gives us a reason to be eternally hopeful.[6] What a powerful promise this is!

Well, once you have hope, you must add faith and action to it. God expects you to 'bell the cat' – so to speak. He expects you to take the initiative towards change. He expects you to initiate the discussion; to wave the peace flag; to reconcile; to forgive; to respond in love; and to care for your spouse.

If you will do your part, care passionately for your spouse, and go beyond the call of duty, you stand a better chance of seeing amazing miracles in your life and marriage than if you don't. Also, irrespective of what eventually happens, you will have the satisfaction of knowing that you did your best and you played your part!

That's all God is asking for and that's all you need to do to give yourself a good foundation for a rock solid marriage.

I trust that you have received some tools to help you win at the 'game' of love. As somebody once said, "Marriage is the only 'game' in the world where both players can either win together or loss together".

Well, I have no doubt that you will chose to win!

"If you obey and serve God, you will spend the rest of your days in prosperity and the rest of your years in contentment." (Job 36:11.) Paraphrased

Finally, if your relationship with God is fractured, it will pay you to get it fixed right away, as this is foundational to everything you've been reading. To have a Rock Solid Marriage, you need a Solid Rock to build on. The scriptures tell us that **Jesus Christ** is that Solid Rock. If you turn your life over to Him, He will surely help you. Visit a vibrant life-giving Church in your area and ask the minister there to help you take the next crucial step.

"... If anyone is in Christ, he is a new creation. The old things have passed away. Behold, all things have become new." (2 Corinthians 5:17.)

1 Philippians 4:19
2 Romans 8:37
3 Romans 5:5
4 Psalm 37:4
5 Philippians 4:13
6 Colossians 1:27

For more books from the Author go to:
www.rocksolidmarriages.com